Read-About

What Is a Thermometer?

By Lisa Trumbauer

Consultants
David Larwa
National Science Consultant

Nanci R. Vargus, Ed.D
Assistant Professor of Literacy
University of Indianapolis
Indianapolis, Indiana

Children's Press®
A Division of Scholastic Inc.
New York   Toronto   London   Auckland   Sydney
Mexico City   New Delhi   Hong Kong
Danbury, Connecticut

Designer: Herman Adler Design
Photo Researcher: Caroline Anderson
The photo on the cover shows a girl reading a thermometer.

Library of Congress Cataloging-in-Publication Data

Trumbauer, Lisa, 1963-
  What is a thermometer? / by Lisa Trumbauer.
    p. cm. — (Rookie read-about science)
Includes index.
Summary: Simple text and photographs describe and illustrate how to use a thermometer.
  ISBN 0-516-22874-9 (lib bdg.)   0-516-24611-9 (pbk.)
  1. Thermometers—Juvenile literature. [1. Thermometers.]
I. Title.
II. Series.
  QC271.4.T78 2003
  681'.2-dc21

                                    2003003906

CHILDREN'S PRESS, and ROOKIE READ-ABOUT®,
and associated logos are trademarks and or registered trademarks
of Scholastic Library Publishing. SCHOLASTIC and associated logos
are trademarks and or registered trademarks of Scholastic Inc.

1 2 3 4 5 6 7 8 9 10 R 12 11 10 09 08 07 06 05 04 03

How do you know how
hot or cold it is outside?

You look at a thermometer.

A thermometer has numbers. The numbers tell you the temperature (TEM-pur-uh-chur).

The temperature is how hot or cold something is.

The temperature is high when something is hot.

It is low when something is cold.

Thermometers measure (MEH-zhur) temperature in degrees.

This is a cold day.

The temperature is low.

Now the snow is gone.
It is a warm day.

Will the temperature be
higher or lower?

What would happen if you put a thermometer outside in a very hot and sunny place?

The temperature would be high.

Thermometers tell temperature in different ways.

This thermometer has a needle. The needle points to the temperature.

This thermometer has a red liquid inside a glass tube. The liquid goes up and down.

Where the liquid stops tells how hot or cold it is.

Some thermometers
show the temperature
with just numbers.

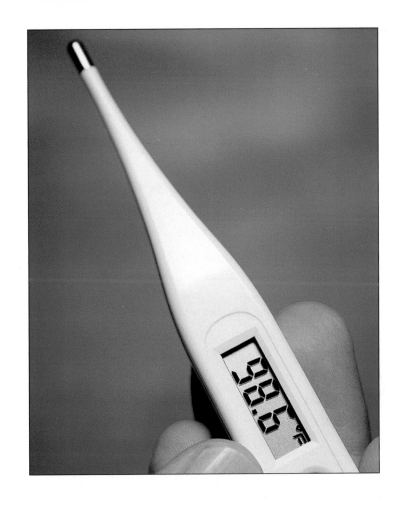

They are called digital (DIJ-uh-tuhl) thermometers.

People use thermometers when they cook.

Some thermometers measure the temperature of meat.

This is a candy thermometer.
It measures the temperature
of liquids.

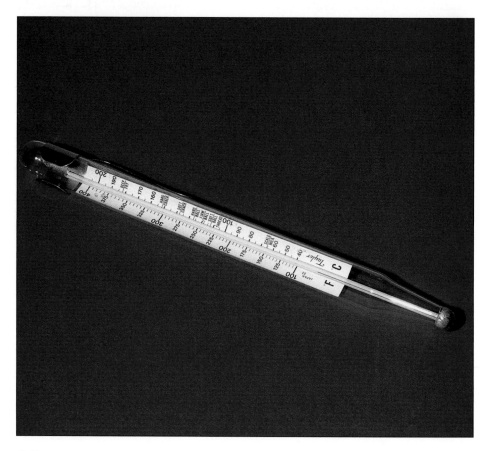

It can tell you when fudge
is done.

Thermometers can also tell you if you are sick.

Your normal body temperature is 98.6 degrees. If your body temperature is too high, you have a fever.

You may have used
a strip thermometer
when you were sick.

You hold the strip
against your forehead.
Your temperature lights
up on the strip.

Let's go outside!

The thermometer will tell us what to wear. Is it hot outside, or cold?

Words You Know

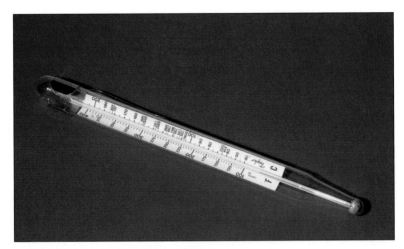

candy thermometer

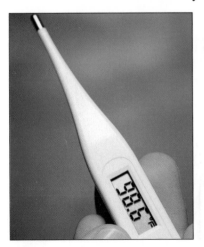

digital thermometer

needle

strip thermometer

thermometer

Index

About the Author

As a student, Lisa Trumbauer found science a mystery. Now the author of nearly two hundred books for children, Lisa enjoys unlocking the mystery of science by writing about it in ways that kids—and she—can understand. Lisa lives in New Jersey with one dog, two cats, and her husband, Dave.

Photo Credits

Photographs © 2003: Dembinsky Photo Assoc.: 8 (Dusan Smetana), 10 (Richard Hamilton Smith); Ellen B. Senisi: cover; Photo Researchers, NY/Stuart Westmorland: 18; PhotoEdit: 29 (Peter Byron), 17, 21 (Tony Freeman), 28 (Michael Newman), 23, 25 (David Young-Wolff); Stock Boston: 3, 5, 14, 30 bottom right, 31 bottom (Bob Daemmrich), 26, 31 top (Stephen Frisch), 6 (Aaron Haupt), 13 (Peter Menzel); Superstock, Inc./Francisco Cruz: 19, 30 bottom left; The Image Works/Kathy McLaughlin: 9; Visuals Unlimited/Erwin C. "Bud" Nielsen: 22, 30 top.